First World War
and Army of Occupation
War Diary
France, Belgium and Germany

41 DIVISION
124 Infantry Brigade
Royal Fusiliers (City of London Regiment)
17th Battalion
1 April 1919 - 30 September 1919

WO95/2643/5

The Naval & Military Press Ltd
www.nmarchive.com
Published in association with The National Archives

Published by

The Naval & Military Press Ltd

Unit 10 Ridgewood Industrial Park,

Uckfield, East Sussex,

TN22 5QE England

Tel: +44 (0) 1825 749494

www.naval-military-press.com

www.nmarchive.com

This diary has been reprinted in facsimile from the original. Any imperfections are inevitably reproduced and the quality may fall short of modern type and cartographic standards.

© Crown Copyright
Images reproduced by permission of The National Archives, London, England, 2015.

Contents

Document type	Place/Title	Date From	Date To
Heading	WO95/2643 (5)		
Heading	London Division (Late 41st Division) 124th Infy Bde 17th Bn Roy. Fusiliers Apr-Sep 1919 From 2 Div 6 Bde		
War Diary	Efrath.	01/04/1919	02/04/1919
War Diary	Refrath	03/04/1919	30/04/1919
War Diary	Bensberg Area.	01/05/1919	12/05/1919
War Diary	Marialinden	13/05/1919	18/06/1919
War Diary	Obr.Vilkerath	19/06/1919	30/06/1919
War Diary	Hoffnung-Sthal	01/07/1919	25/08/1919
War Diary	Overath	26/08/1919	21/09/1919
War Diary	Neun-Kirchen	22/09/1919	30/09/1919

WD95/2643(5)

WD95/2643(5)

LONDON DIVISION
(LATE 41ST DIVISION)
124TH INFY BDE

17TH BN ROY. FUSILIERS
APR - SEP 1919

FROM 2 DIV
6 Bde

WAR DIARY
or
INTELLIGENCE SUMMARY.
(Erase heading not required.)

Army Form C. 2118.

Place	Date	Hour	Summary of Events and Information	Remarks and references to Appendices
EFRATH.	April.1st.		Training by Coys,P.T.,& Musketry.& Education.	
			Officers joining:- 2/Lieut.E.J.Robinson.from 109th Light Trench Mortar Battery.	
	2nd.		Coys engaged on re-organisation and Preparition for absorption of drafts.	
			Act of Courage: from 2nd Army Routine Orders:-	
			"The Army Commander wishes to express his appreciation of the following Act of Courage:- On Feb.12th 1919.No.2717.Pte Gladman.H.L. and No.77853.Pte.C.E.Birdseye.17th Royal Fusiliers. were passing a skating pond at DIEFENTHAL near LEICHLINGEN,when the ice gave way and a man and a women went through.	
			These soldiers without hesitation,and while the other people were fleeing from the dangerous proximity of the hole,went to the assistance of the man and women who were clinging to the edge of the ice in the hole.By joining their belts together they were able to reach them and effect their rescue.There is every probability that the people would have been drowned had it not been for the prompt and courageous action of Ptes.Gladman and Birdeyes.	
			A record of the above will be made in the Regimental Conduct Sheets of Ptes Gladman and Birdeyes.In accordance with Kings Regs.Para.1919 (XIV)"	
			Officers joining:- Major.(A/Lieut.Col.)M.O.Clarke.D.S.O. (Authy.3rd Army No.A/A/2685./1.).	

Army Form C. 2118.

WAR DIARY
or
INTELLIGENCE SUMMARY.
(Erase heading not required.)

Place	Date	Hour	Summary of Events and Information	Remarks and references to Appendices
REFRATH.	April.3rd.		51st.Battn.Royal Fusiliers.arrived at station and were absorbed as a draft:- strength in Other Ranks:- 717.	
			Major.(A/Lieut.Col)M.O.Clarke.D.S.O.assumes command of the Battalion as from this date.	
			Officers joining from the 51st Battn.Royal Fusiliers.	
			Lieut.Col.A.E.Sulman.M.C. Major.T.A.Armstrong. Capt.G.F.Rickett.	
			Capt.E.H.Davis. Capt.F.L.Jones.M.C. Lt/A/Capt.W.V.Aston.	
			Lieut.J.R.S.Bramer. Lt/A/Capt.W.F.Mair. Lieut.B.J.Finnie.M.C.	
			Lt.A/Capt.W.J.Hood M.C. Lieut.C.W.Field. Lieut.A.W.Mackenzie.	
			Lieut.W.E.Cooper. Lt.A/Capt.H.W.Brookling.M.C. Lieut.C.G.Gann.	
			Lieut.A.Mason. Lieut.F.J.Williams. Lieut.C.A.Brasher.	
			" E.C.Hudson. G.H.Brumwin. " A.E.Ball.	
			" C.T.Davis.M.M. " A.E.Wells. " F.E.Hankin.	
			2/Lt.W.W.Line. 2/Lt.A/Capt.P.Draper. 2/Lt.P.W.Organ.	
			" G.F.Stearn. " W.E.Chapman. " J.A.Hough.	
			" A.J.Dixon. " E.Harris. " F.Swain.	
			" E.G.Andrews.M.C. " E.I.Freemantle.M.C. 2/Lt.J.F.Rogers.	
			" P.S.Wicks. " H.G.Reynolds. " H.P.Sheppard.	
			" R.V.Macdonald.D.C.M. " E.Coleman. " J.L.Palmer.	
			" G.A.Liddiard.M.M. " V.L.Barclay. " J.N.C.McGregory.	
			Lieut.Barratt. Capt.the Rev.J.Meeham. Capt.N.Lawsom.M.C. (R.A.M.C.)	

Army Form C. 2118.

WAR DIARY
or
INTELLIGENCE SUMMARY.
(Erase heading not required.)

Instructions regarding War Diaries and Intelligence Summaries are contained in F. S. Regs., Part II. and the Staff Manual respectively. Title pages will be prepared in manuscript.

Place	Date	Hour	Summary of Events and Information	Remarks and references to Appendices
REFRATH.	April.4th.		Coys engaged on re-organisation.	[signature]
			Officers leaving th Battalion for Demobilization. Lieut.S.W.CHANCELLOR. 2/Lieuts.J.W.JAMES. E.WILKINSON. W.S.WAY. W.B.HOLLAND. E.W.PATRICK Bushnell.W.R.WEBB. A.E.MAY. E.W.DIXON.T.H.BENNETT.178 Other Ranks.left the Battalion for demobilization.	[signature]
	5th.		Coys engaged on re-organisation and training (P.T.)	[signature]
	6th.		Church Parades.	[signature]
	7th.		Coys training according to programme attached hereto. Officers proceeding to duty at Brigade School of Instruction:- Major.J.A.Armstrong.(Commandant.) 2/Lieut.(A/Capt.)P.Draper. Lieut.E.W.Cooper.	[signature]
	8th.		Coy Training.No.114631.P.S.M. P.J.Comerford was awarded the M.S.M. in the New Year Honours Despatch.(Authy: London Gazette 18/1/19.)	[signature]
	9th.		Officers leaving the Battalion. Capt.J.Lawson. (R.A.M.C.) Coy Training according to programme attached hereto.	[signature]
	10th		Coy training according to programme attached hereto. Officers leaving the Battalion for demobilization:-2/Lieut. E.M.Cooke. 11 Other Ranks left the Battalion for demobilization.	[signature]
	11th		Coy training according to programme attached hereto. Officer leaving the Battalion to be attached to London Division H.Q. as a Demobilization Officer:- Lieut.G.H.BRUWIN. Officer leaving the Battalion,Capt.J.MEEHAN.(The Rev.) M.C.	[signature]
	12th		Parades in accordance with programme. Officers leaving the Battalion for demobilization.2/Lieut.A.Easson.11 Other Ranks left for demobilization.	[signature]
	13th		Church Parades.	[signature]

Army Form C. 2118.

WAR DIARY
or
INTELLIGENCE SUMMARY.
(Erase heading not required.)

Place	Date	Hour	Summary of Events and Information	Remarks and references to Appendices
BEFORTH.	April.14th.		Training as per programme. Officers leaving for demobilization:- Capt.C.H.Hewitt.2/Lieut.H.S.Gill. 7 Other Ranks left for demobilization.	
	15th		Training as per Programme.	
	16th		Two Companies cutting wood and brushwood. Remainder training as per programme. Officer joining:- Major.C.P.GRIFFITHS.C.F.	
	17th		Two Companies cutting wood and brushwood. Remainder training as per programme.	
	18th		Church Parades. 8 Officers and 100 Other Ranks proceeded up the Rhine from Cologne to ANDERNACH and back. 3 Other Ranks left the Battalion for demobilization.	

Army Form C. 2118.

WAR DIARY
or
INTELLIGENCE SUMMARY.
(Erase heading not required.)

Place	Date	Hour	Summary of Events and Information	Remarks and references to Appendices
REFRATH.	April.19th.		Two half Companies cutting wood and brushwood. Remainder training as per programme. Officers leaving. Lieut.Col.A.E.SULMAN M.C. 14 Other Ranks left for demobilization. Ration Strength:- Officers.67. Other Ranks.1,260.	
REFRATH.	20th		Church Parades.	
	21st.		Training as per programme.	
	22nd		Major.General.Sir.S.T.N.Lawford.K.C.B., Commanding LONDON DIVISION accompanies by Brig.General PERCY.inspected the Battalion on Parade, and inspected billets at REFRATH and BENSBERG. Parade State:-	

```
                    Officers.        Other Ranks.

         On Parade.     41.              965.
         Regt.Employ.    3.              182.
         On Command.                     164.
         On Leave.      13.               97.
                       ----              ----
                        57.             1408.
                       ====              ====
```

WAR DIARY
or
INTELLIGENCE SUMMARY.
(Erase heading not required.)

Army Form C. 2118.

Place	Date	Hour	Summary of Events and Information	Remarks and references to Appendices
REFRATH.	April. 23rd.		Training in accordance with programme. Officers leaving the Battalion to join the 104th Prisoner of War Company:- Lieut.F.O.Parry. 2/Lieut.G.S.B.Metheringham. M.M. Officers leaving for demobilization. Major.S.J.M.Hole.M.C. Lieut.A.E.Ball. 2/Lieut.G.F.Hilton. 2/Lieut.J.Mills. 12 Other Ranks left the Battalion for demobilization.	
	24th		Training in accordance with programme.	
	25th		"A" & "C" Coys moved from billets into quarters at the SCHLOSS.NENSBERG. "B" & "D" Coys training in accordance with programme. The following copy of Divisional Order was published in Battalion Orders. "No Officer or Man will walk about singly after dark"	
	26th		Training in accordance with programme. Officers leaving the Battalion for demobilization:- 2/Lieut.V.L.Barcley.2/Lt.S.N.E.Davis. 1 Other Rank left the Battalion for demobilization. Ration Strength:- 69 Officers 1106.Other Ranks.	
	27th		Church Parares.	
	28th		Training in accordance with programme,but ceased at 12.00 hrs to allow all ranks to attend London Divisional Race Meeting.	
	29th		Training in accordance with programme,but ceased at 12.00 hours to allow all ranks to attend London Divisional Race Meeting.	
	30th		Training in accordance with programme.	

Army Form C. 2118.

WAR DIARY
or
INTELLIGENCE SUMMARY.
(Erase heading not required.)

Instructions regarding War Diaries and Intelligence Summaries are contained in F. S. Regs., Part II. and the Staff Manual respectively. Title pages will be prepared in manuscript.

Place	Date	Hour	Summary of Events and Information	Remarks and references to Appendices
BENSBERG AREA.	May 1st.		"C" Coy. was on special duty as "Inlying Picquet" in case of German disturbances. All quiet. Train Guard sent for Eifel Tower Guard.	
	" 2nd.		"B" Coy. and Lewis Guns of "A" & "C" Coys. on range at BRUCK. Weather fine.	
	" 3rd.		"B" & "D" Coys. on range. Lieut.L.C.Doncaster went on leave.	
	" 4th.		Commanding Officer, Capt.Chapman & Adjutant motored to Marielinden (23rd Middlesex) to go round Front Area.	
	" 5th.		Battalion practised ceremonial on field at Frankenforst at 10.30 hrs. Capt.Leander proceeded on special leave to edit to "Golden Horseshoe".	
	" 6th.		The Commander-in-Chief (General Robertson) inspected the 3rd London Infantry Brigade on Exerzier Platz at 11.00 hrs. Brigade formed up in line – full marching order.	
	" 7th.		"A" & "C" Coys. on range at BRUCK. 8 officers and 200 Other Ranks went on Rhine Trip. Coy. Commanders' Conference at 17.00 hrs.	41
	" 8th.		A Guard of Honour of 3 Officers and 100 Other Ranks commanded by Capt.G.P.Chapman,O.B.E.,M.C. was sent to VIth Corps H.Q. for the Duke of Connaught. Highly congratulated by Brigade Commander. Lorry took Coy.Commanders to Forward Area. 65 complete sets of tent-boards suddenly arrived at Frankenforst. Major W.C.Smith.D.S.O. M.C. proceeded to assume duty as 2nd-in-Command to 20th Bn. K.R.R.Corps.	
	" 9th.		"D" Coy. started to erect camp on ground near Frankenforst, 100 tents being sent. Capt.G.P.Chapman.O.B.E.,M.C. took over duties as 2nd-in-Command	
	" 10th.		Camp at Frankenforst completed, as regards tents being pitched. Lieut-Colonel Clarke.D.S.O. went to stay with Brig-General Jackson, of 2nd Eastern Brigade.	
	" 11th.		C.O. of 23rd Bn. Middlesex Regt. came to look round our Bensberg billets and left at 15.00 hrs. Lovely weather.	

Army Form C. 2118.

WAR DIARY
or
INTELLIGENCE SUMMARY.
(Erase heading not required.)

Instructions regarding War Diaries and Intelligence Summaries are contained in F. S. Regs., Part II. and the Staff Manual respectively. Title pages will be prepared in manuscript.

Place	Date	Hour	Summary of Events and Information	Remarks and references to Appendices
BENSBERG AREA.	May 12th.		At 11.00 hrs. C.O. returned from 2nd Eastern Brigade. Coy.Commanders' Conference at 15.00 Hrs. 2/Lieut.Carson went on leave.	
MARIA-LINDEN.	13th.		The Battalion, less "D" Coy., moved by train from Bensberg at 07.00 hrs. to Overath to take over from 23rd Middlesex Regt. "D" Coy. proceeded by 12 lorries to Drabenderhohe. Train arrived at Overath at 07.45 hrs. A,B, & C Coys. breakfasted at station and then moved off to the relief. A & H.Q. Coys. billetted in Marialinden, B Coy. at Landwehr, C Coy. (right out post Coy) at Grutzenbach, and D Coy. at Drabenderhohe. Relief complete by 15.00 hrs. Weather very fine. Capt.D.G.Gibson,M.C. returned from leave and took over duties as 2nd-in-Command from Capt.Chapman.O.B.E.,M.C. who proceeded on leave.	
	14th.		G.O.C. Brigade called at Battn.H.Q. 46 tents arrived. All Coys. settling down and cleaning billets.	
	15th.		Commanding Officer visited all Coys.	
	16th.		ALBUERA DAY. (no parades). Record of Regt. read out to all troops. Games and concerts by all Coys.	
	17th.		Conference at Brigade H.Q. at 11.45 hrs.	
	18th.		Hot and a very quiet day. 2/Lieut.H.R.Moxon and 12 other ranks left for demobilization	
	19th.		Parades as usual. A & B Coys. route march.	
	20th.		Coys. parade in shirt sleeves for first time. Weather very hot.	
	21st.		"A" Coy. bathed.	
	22nd.		Training under Coy. arrangements. H.Q.Coy. beat A Coy. at cricket.	
	23rd.		"B" Coy. went to bathe at Overath.	
	24th.		Aquatic Sports in river for A,B, & H.Q.Coys. The Bde.Commander attended.	

Army Form C. 2118.

WAR DIARY
or
INTELLIGENCE SUMMARY.
(Erase heading not required.)

Instructions regarding War Diaries and Intelligence Summaries are contained in F. S. Regs., Part II. and the Staff Manual respectively. Title pages will be prepared in manuscript.

Place	Date	Hour	Summary of Events and Information	Remarks and references to Appendices
MARIA-LINDEN.	May 25th.		15 Officers went on Rhine Trip. Weather very fine. 8 men transferred to Labour Battalion.	
"	26th.		R.E's called to make arrangements about putting up huts for H.Q. at Marialinden, & B Coy.	
"	27th.		B Coy. relieved D Coy. at D rabenderhohe, all completed by 15.00 hrs. 3 lorries used for the move.	
"	28th.		A Coy. relieved C Coy. in Right Forward Area by 15.00 hrs. Two Lorries used.	
"	29th.		35 men sent to 36th C.C.S. for attachment, 8 to Searchlight Section, & 8 to Divl.Train. Very fine lecture given, "In the Grip of the German Occupation in Russia".	
"	30th.		Very hot. 17th R.Fusiliers beat the 23rd R.F. at cricket.	
"	31st		Four civilian prisoners captured: 2 from A Coy.right front. 2 from B Coy.Landwehr. 17th R.Fusiliers played 53rd Brigade R.G.A. football, lost 3-1.	
	June 1st.		Capt.Boult proceeded on leave to United Kingdom. 3 civil prisoners captured by A Coy. (3 male and 2 female). 2/Lieuts.Miles and Gillett returned from leave.	
"	2nd.		2/Lieut.Carson returned from leave.	
"	3rd.		King's Birthday. Ceremonial Parade at 09.00 hrs. Holiday. 1 civilian captured by A Coy. 5 civilians arrested by B Coy.	
"	4th.		C,D, & H.Q. Coys. inspected by Corps Commander. Capt.Rickett reported back from leave.	
"	5th.		1 civilian arrested by A Coy. 100 men proceeded as draft to 25th Middlesex Regt.	
"	6th.		Lieut-Col.Clarke.D.S.O. proceeded on leave. Capt.Gibson.M.C. took over command of Battalion. Lieut-Colonel Clarke.D.S.O. made Brevet Lieut-Colonel, and Capt.Gwinnell awarded M.C. in King's Birthday Honours.	
"	7th.		Capt.Chapman returned from leave and took over command of the Battalion.	

(3972) Wt W355/P360 604000 12/17 D.D.& L. Sch.53a- Forms/C2118/15

Army Form C. 2118.

WAR DIARY
or
INTELLIGENCE SUMMARY.

(Erase heading not required.)

Instructions regarding War Diaries and Intelligence Summaries are contained in F.S. Regs., Part II. and the Staff Manual respectively. Title pages will be prepared in manuscript.

Place	Date	Hour	Summary of Events and Information	Remarks and references to Appendices
MARIA-LINDEN.	June May 8th.		Open air church parade service. C,D, & H.Q.Coys. attended.	
"	9th.		Whit Monday. Holiday.	
"	10th.		Lieut.Line proceeded on leave.	
"	11th.		Two civilians captured by B Coy. Cricket match between 17th R.Fusiliers and 190th Battn. R.F.A. 17th R.Fusiliers won by 1 wicket.	
"	12th.		Two civilians captured by B Coy. G.O.C. visited Left Coy.Sector. (B Coy.)	
"	13th.		Lieut.Finnie proceeded on leave.	
"	14th.		Lieut.Brookling proceeded on leave.	
"	15th.		Parade service for church, open air. C,D, & H.Q.Coys. attended. One civilian captured by B Coy.	
"	16th.		One civilian captured by A Coy.	
"	17th.		Lieut.Hough proceeded on leave. Coy.Commanders' Conference at Battn. H.Q.	
"	18th.		All surplus stores packed and sent to OVERATH. Capt.Rickett, Lieuts.Brasher and Williams, and 2/Lieut.Macdonald proceeded to Depot at OVERATH. Coy.Commanders' Conference at Batta.H.Q.	
OBR.VILKE-RATH.	19th.		H.Q.,C, & D Coys. moved to OBR.VILKERATH at 07.15 hrs. Battn. H.Q. opened at OBR.VILKERATH at 09.00 hrs. H.Q., C, & D Coys. camped in tents. Lieut-Col.Clarke.D.S.O. returned from leave and resumed command of the Battalion. Capt.Gibson relinquished duties as 2nd-in-Command of the Battalion and took over command of "C" Coy.	
"	20th.		Lieuts.Line, Finnie, and Hough returned from leave.	
"	21st.		Lieut.Brookling and 2/Lieut.Goodier returned from leave. Capt.Chapman.O.B.E.,M.C. appointed Actg/Major whilst acting as 2nd-in-Command. G.O.C. visited C.O.	
"	22nd.		Capt.Boult.M.C. returned from leave.	

WAR DIARY
or
INTELLIGENCE SUMMARY.

(Erase heading not required.)

Army Form C. 2118.

Place	Date	Hour	Summary of Events and Information	Remarks and references to Appendices
OBR.VILKERATH.	June 23rd.		Brigade Aquatic Sports held at KLEF.	
"	24th.		Lieut.-Col.Ashburner.D.S.O. toured front line Posts with Lieut.Col.M.C.Clarke.D.S.O.	
"	25th.		Lieut.-Col.Clarke.D.S.O. proceeded on leave to United Kingdom. Major Chapman.O.B.E.,M.C. assumed command of Battalion.	
"	26th.		Capt.Fld des, R.A.M.C. M.O. to 17th Bn. R.Fusiliers, proceeded to join 47th General Hospital, BONN. Lieut.O'Neil, R.A.M.C. took over as M.O. to the Battalion.	
"	27th.		A & B Coys. relieved from Front Line Posts by C & D Coys. 23rd Bn. Royal Fusiliers. A & B Coys. moved into camp at OVERATH.	
"	28th.		Lieut.Finnie proceeded on leave. PEACE signed.	
"	29th.		C,D, & H.Q.Coys. attended open air church parade at OBR.VILKERATH with Band.	
"	30th.		Advance party of 1 Officer and 4 N.C.Os. per Coy. proceeded to HOFFNUNGSTHAL.	

COMMANDING 17TH (SERVICE) BATTN.
THE ROYAL FUSILIERS

WAR DIARY
or
INTELLIGENCE SUMMARY.
(Erase heading not required.)

Army Form C. 2118.

Place	Date	Hour	Summary of Events and Information	Remarks and references to Appendices
HOFFNUNG-STHAL.	July 1st.		Battn. moved into HOFFNUNGSTHAL, & VOLBERG 09.00 hrs. B & D Coys. in billets, A & C in tents.	
"	2nd.		Coys. at disposal of Coy.Commanders for interior economy. Lieut.Goodier proceeded on leave to United Kingdom.	
"	3rd.		Holiday on account of the Signing of Peace.	
"	4th.		Coys. carried out Training Programme. "B" Coy. on range.	
"	5th.		Coys. at disposal of Coy.Commanders. Cricket Match between Bn. Officers & N.C.Os. Two 77 m.m. German guns captured by the 17th Royal Fusiliers forwarded to Depot in ENGLAND. Bn. advised by War Office.	
"	6th.		Church services for the Battn. in VOLBERG Parish Church.	
"	7th.		Parades according to programme. Lewis Gunners on range.	
"	8th.		Battn. Library opened at HOFFNUNGSTHAL. Cafes and Restaurants opened to all ranks until 22.00 hrs. Tattoo extended to 22.30 hrs. Adjutant's parade on parade ground.	
"	9th.		Paraded according to programme. "B" Coy. on range.	
"	10th.		Bn. Route March cancelled owing to bad weather. Education and interior economy. 2/Lieut.Gillett proceeded on method course of languages at VIth Corps.	
"	12th.		Parades as per programme. Sum of £77-16-0 collected by the Battalion for the Royal Fusiliers Memorial Fund. Lieut.Laver joined the Battn. from the Middlesex Regt. and was posted to "A" Coy.	
"	13th.		Church service held in VOLBERG Parish Church.	

Army Form C. 2118.

WAR DIARY
or
INTELLIGENCE SUMMARY.
(Erase heading not required.)

Instructions regarding War Diaries and Intelligence Summaries are contained in F. S. Regs., Part II. and the Staff Manual respectively. Title pages will be prepared in manuscript.

Place	Date	Hour	Summary of Events and Information	Remarks and references to Appendices
HOFFNUNG-STHAL.	July 13th		Sports in afternoon. Brig-General Percy C.B.,C.M.G.,D.S.O. attended.	
"	14th		Lieut.Bramer proceeded to Division to take over duties of Divl.Sports Officer, temporarily. Lieut.Col.Clarke,D.S.O. returned from leave. The following 2/Lieuts. Become Lieuts:- 2/Lieut.Line. 2/Lieut.Swain. 2/Lieut.Harris. 2/Lieut.Carson. 2/Lieu t.Goodier.	
"	15th		Sports concluded in afternoon. Brig.General Percy,C.B.,C.M.G. presented prizes. "A" Coy. won Coy.Cup.	
"	16th		Inspection by Divl.Commander at 10.00 hours. Dress: Fighting Order. The Battalion billets and transport were inspected. 2/Lieut.Fairbank joined the Battalion from ENGLAND. 11 N.C.Os. and men joined Battn. from 40th R.Fusiliers.	
"	17th		Parades as per Training Programme. Cricket match with 23rd Royal Fusiliers at HOFFNUNGSTHAL.	
"	18th		Coy.Commanders' Conference at Battn.H.Q. Parades according to programme. "A" Coy. and Lewis Gunners on range.	
"	19th		Holiday for Peace Celebration.	
"	20th		Church service in VOLBERG Parish Church. Cricket match with 23rd Royal Fusiliers at OVERATH. Lieut.Goodier returned from leave. 7 men joined from 5th Bn. R.Fusiliers.	
"	21st		"B" Coy. and Lewis Gunners on range. Parades according to Training Programme.	
"	22nd		Parades according to Training Programme.	

Army Form C. 2118.

WAR DIARY
or
INTELLIGENCE SUMMARY.

(Erase heading not required.)

Instructions regarding War Diaries and Intelligence Summaries are contained in F. S. Regs., Part II. and the Staff Manual respectively. Title pages will be prepared in manuscript.

Place	Date	Hour	Summary of Events and Information	Remarks and references to Appendices
HOFFNUNG- ST HAL.	July 23rd.		Lieut.Firmie returned from leave. "B" Coy. on range.	
"	24th.		C.O. inspected "B" Coy. in Coy.Drill Competitions at 10.00 hrs. "D" Coy. on range.	
"	25th.		Coy.Drill Competition, "A" Coy. 10.00 hrs. Training for other Coys. as per programme.	
"	26th.		"C" & "D" Coys. inspected in Coy.Drill Competition. Won by "B" Coy. "A" Coy. on Bayonet Fighting Course. "B" Coy. on range. Lieut-Col.Clarke.D.S.O. proceeded to U.K. on special leave.	
"	27th.		Church Parade service in VOLBERG Parish Church. Lieut.Line returned from leave.	
"	28th.		"B" Coy. inspected by G.O.C. for Brigade Drill Competition. Parades for other Coys. as per programme.	
"	29th.		Lieut.Hood proceeded on leave. Brigade Sports held at KLEF. Brigade Cup won by 17th R.Fusiliers. Parades finished at 11.00 hours.	
"	30th.		Brigade Horse Show. Parades finished 11.00 hours.	
"	31st		Parades as per Training Programme. Lieut-Colonel M.C.Clarke.D.S.O. returned from leave.	

Army Form C. 2118.

WAR DIARY
or
INTELLIGENCE SUMMARY.
(Erase heading not required.)

Instructions regarding War Diaries and Intelligence Summaries are contained in F. S. Regs., Part II. and the Staff Manual respectively. Title pages will be prepared in manuscript.

Place	Date	Hour	Summary of Events and Information	Remarks and references to Appendices
Hoffnungsthal	August. 1st.		Route March.A,B,& C.Coys in fighting order. Cricket Match against 19th Middlesex. Won by 41 runs. System of Pay & Mess books started in Battalion.	
	2nd.		Coy's at disposal of Coys Commanders for issue of new clothing.	
	3rd.		Church Parade service in Volberg parish Church. Warning from Brigade to be prepared to move to back area on the 6th inst.	
	4th.		Bank Holiday. Lt.Brasher proceeded on leave. Warning Order of 3rd Cancelled.Orders to relieve 2/4 Queens Regt of guards etc,in Cologne on 5th inst.	
	5th.		9 Officers 234 Other Ranks proceeded by lorries to meet guides at Haus Frankenforst to relieve guards in Cologne. Lieut.Gann proceeded on Leave. Lieut.Hough returned from leave.	
	6th.		Lt.Rogers proceeded on leave. Lt.Hough left Battn to join Chinese Labour Corps. Noyelles,France. Lt.Brookling returned from leave.	
	7th.		C.O. Adjt. & 4 Coy Commdrs made preliminary reconnaissance of Overath area. Lieut.Hudson proceeded on leave.	
	8th.		Lt.Liddiard proceeded on leave.Promulgation of finding of court martial on Lt.Plant. About 4 hours after promulgation Lt.Plant found in billet suffering from Gun Shot Wound in head. Cricket match against 11th Bn.Queens. Won. Lt.Hankin proceeded on leave.	42W
	9th.		Lieut.Mason proceeded on leave. Court of Enquiry on Death of Lt.Plant. "Finding "Suicide whilst of unsound mind."	
	10th.		Lt.Williams proceeded on leave. "B"Coys billet lent to Civil Authorities from 14.00 hrs to 20.00 hrs. Water Polo match.	
	11th.		Lt.Reynolds, & Lt.Wells proceeded on leave.Lts Miles & Swain relieved these Officers at Kalk. Lecture by Capt.Roberts on "What we have won for the world"in cinema.	

Army Form C. 2118.

WAR DIARY
or
INTELLIGENCE SUMMARY.
(Erase heading not required.)

Instructions regarding War Diaries and Intelligence Summaries are contained in F. S. Regs., Part II. and the Staff Manual respectively. Title pages will be prepared in manuscript.

Place	Date	Hour	Summary of Events and Information	Remarks and references to Appendices
Hoffnungsthal. August.	12th.		Lieut.Dixin proceeded on leave.	
	13th.		Lieut Ashwell & Field proceeded on leave. Coys at disposal of Coys Commdrs.	
	14th.		Lieut.Brothers & Lieut.Hickman. proceeded on leave. Move to Overath postponed from 19th (approx) to 25th August.	
	15th.		Capt.Gwinnell & 2/Lieut.West proceeded on leave.Lt.Col.M.C.Clarke.D.S.O.proceeded to join 3rd Bn. Royal Fusiliers at Hounslow. Major.G.P.Chapman.O.B.E.,M.C. took over command of the Battalion.	
	16th.		Lieut.Munford proceeded on leave.	
	17th.		Church Parade service,in Volberg Parish Church. Officers Rhine Trip. Officers on trip proceeded by lorry to Bonn. Sheppard	
	18th.		Lieut. proceeded on leave.Coys at disposal of Coy Commdrs.Lt.Finnie proceeded on leave.	
	19th.		Lieut.Miles.proceeded on leave.	
	20th.		Guards found at Kalk returned to Battalion.	
	21st.		Capt.D.G.Gibson.M.C. proceeded on leave. Brigade Rifle meeting at Overath.	
	22nd.		Brigade Rifle meeting continued.Bde Cup for Rifle Meeting Won by 17th Bn.Royal Fusiliers. 1 Man proceeded to United Kingdom for Demobilization.	
	23rd.		Lieut.Rogers reported from leave.2/Lt.Macdonald D.C.M. retained at G.H.Q.General & Commercial School and ceases to be on Education Officer of this Battalion.	
	24th.		Open air Church Parade on Battn Cricket Ground.	
	25th.		C & D Coys moved to Overath. Court of enquiry assembled to enquire into the loss of a registered Letter.	

Army Form C. 2118.

WAR DIARY
or
INTELLIGENCE SUMMARY.
(Erase heading not required.)

Instructions regarding War Diaries and Intelligence Summaries are contained in F. S. Regs., Part II. and the Staff Manual respectively. Title pages will be prepared in manuscript.

Place	Date	Hour	Summary of Events and Information	Remarks and references to Appendices
Overath. August.	26th.		"A" "B" & "H" "Q" Coys moved to Overath. Headquarters opened at Overath at 10.00 hours. Lieut.Williams returned from leave.	
	27th.		Lieut.Doncaster.M.V. proceeded on leave. "D"Company commenced firing G.M.C.	
	28th.		Capt.Jones.proceeded on leave.Lts Gann.Wells,& Reynolds returned from leave. "Act of Courage" from G.R.O.No.87.of August 27th 1919.by Gen.Sir.W.Robertson. C of C. "On August 1st an officer while swimming in the Rhine at Bonn contrary to orders. got into difficulties and was disappering under the water for the last time. No.68667.Pte.R,Amos 17th Bn.Royal Fusiliers,jumped into the river and swam with the officer to where help was forthcoming and through his efforts the officer was saved. A record of the above will be made in the Regt Conduct Sheet of Pte Amos in accordance with Kings Regulations para.1919 (XIV)	
	29th.		Capt.Rickett proceeded on leave.	
	30th.		Lieut.Boult proceeded on leave. Lieut.Hankin returned from leave.	
	31st.		Lieut's Brothers Dixon & Hickman returned from leave.	

Major.
Commanding 17th Battalion.Royal Fusiliers.

WAR DIARY or INTELLIGENCE-SUMMARY

Army Form C. 2118.

Place	Date	Hour	Summary of Events and Information September 1919	Remarks and references to Appendices
OVERATH.	1919. Sept. 1st.		Divl. Sports Meeting at POLA WIESEN, COLOGNE. "C". Coy. firing G.M.C.	Na
"	2nd.		Lieut. Ashwell returned from leave.	Na
"	3rd.		Rev. H. Holden returned from leave.	Na
"	4th.		Lt-Col. B.L. Montgomery. D.S.O. joined from G.H.Q. & took over command of the Battalion.	Na
"	5th.		Capt. Gwinnell and Lieut. Sheppard returned from leave.	Na
"	6th.		3 Officers (Lts. Swain, Brasher, & Reynolds) & 50 Other Ranks proceeded to U.K. on demobilization.	Na
"	7th.		Church Parade services in Church Army Hut, OVERATH. Capt. Gibson.M.C. returned from leave. Lieut. Harris & 16 Other Ranks proceeded to Drove to participate in Army Rifle Meeting.	Na
"	8th.		Lieut. Carson returned from leave. A & B Coys. commenced G.M.C. Lts. Brookling & West & 40 Other Ranks demobilized.	Na
"	9th.		Major Chapman. O.B.E., M.C. proceeded on leave. Major Griffiths.S.C.F. proceeded on leave.	Na
"	10th.		Brig-General Howard visited Battn. and saw "D" Coy. in course of week's field training.	Na
"	11th.		Lts. Finnie, Miles, Brownlee, & Goodier returned from leave.	Na
"	12th.		Lieut. Doncaster returned from leave.	Na
"	13th.		Capt. Jones.M.C. returned from leave. Football Match, Right v. Left Half Battn.	Na
"	14th.		Open air Church Parade Service.	Na
"	15th.		Capt. Rickett and Lieut. Everard returned from leave.	Na

Army Form C. 2118.

WAR DIARY
or
INTELLIGENCE SUMMARY.
(Erase heading not required.)

Instructions regarding War Diaries and Intelligence Summaries are contained in F.S. Regs., Part II. and the Staff Manual respectively. Title pages will be prepared in manuscript.

Place	Date	Hour	Summary of Events and Information	Remarks and references to Appendices
OVERATH.	1919. Sept.16th.		Divl. Horse Show. Holiday. Lieut.Gillett proceeded to U.K. for demobilization.	M.a
"	17th.		"B" Coy. finished firing G.M.C. Warning order received that Battn. might have to move on Monday, 22nd Sept. Lieut.Williams proceeded on demobilization.	M.a
"	18th.		General Robertson held conference with Brigadier and C.O's of Brigade in Bt.-Col. Montgomery's billet. C.O., Adjt., 2nd i/c, and O.C. "D" Coy., visited line to be taken over. 2/Lieut. G.A.Liddiard.M.M. proceeded to U.K. for demobilization.	M.a
"	19th.		Training in accordance with week's field training. Brig-General Howard visited Battn. and saw "D" Coy. in course of week's field training. Battn.Cross Country Run started at 17.30 hrs. (277 starters). "C" Coy. won 10,483 points "A" Coy. finished G.M.C. 2/Lieut.P.S.Wicks proceeded on leave.	M.a
"	20th.		Os.C. A, B, C & H.Q. Coys, with Transport Officer & Q.M., visited line to be taken over. Football Match between Battn. and 26th R.Fus. Battn. won 4-2. "C" Bty. 190 Bde.R.F.A. Battn. Church Service in Mess Huts. Football Match between Battn. & "C" Bty. 190 Bde.R.F.A. Battn. won 4-0.	M.a
"	21st.		Church Service in Mess Huts.	M.a
NEUN-KIRCHEN.	22nd.		The Battn., less "D" Coy., marched to NEU NKIRCHEN to take over from 23rd R.Fus. "D" Coy. proceeded by 9 lorries to OBR HEISTER & took over the left outposts. 2 platoons of "B" Coy. took over the Right Posts. Battn.H.Q., A, B, & C Coys., & H.Q. Coy. billets in Neun-kirchen. Battn. arrived at 15.30 hrs. Relief complete at 17.00 hrs.	M.er
"	23rd.		C.O. visited "D" Coy. in the outpost line. Lieut.Mason proceeded to U.K. for demobilization. "A" Coy. were inoculated. Inter-platoon knock-out football competition started. 10 platoon "C" Coy. played 12 platoon "C" Coy. 10 platoon won 4-1.	M.a
"	24th.		Brig-Gen. Howard and Bde.Major visited Battn. & inspected the outpost line. "B" Coy. & H.Q. were inoculated. Battn. played cricket match against 41st M.G.C. at HEUMAR. Battn. won by 25 runs.	M.a
"	25th.		Training in accordance with training programme. "C" Coy. had a holiday to Bonn & Cologne as a prize for winning the Battn. Cross Country Run. Major Chapman.O.B.E.,M.C. & Major Griffiths.S.C.F. returned from leave.	M.a
"	26th.		Training as per training programme. "C" Coy. inoculated & Baths in afternoon. No.2 platoon met No.3 platoon in the platoon knock-out competition. A.2 won 10-0.	M.a
"	27th.		Training in accordance with training programme. 2 officer patrols visited villages in front of posts; all was in order. "D" Coy. caught one prisoner trying to pass through post at STEIN. Battn. played 10th Queen's at football in the Kalk Shield. Battn. won 4-1.	M.a
"	28th.		Church Parade in Y.M.C.A. hut. Weekly cross country run took place at 15.00 hrs.; "C" Coy. won. Rained hard all day. Coy. Commanders' Conference after Church Service.	M.a

WAR DIARY.

Army Form C.2118.

Place.	Date.	Summary of Events & Information.	Remarks.
NEUN-KIRCHEN.	1919. Sept.29th.	Training as per training programme. "A" Coy. on the range.	MM
"	30th.	Training as per training programme. "B" Coy. on the range. C.O. visited "D" Coy. in the outpost line. Hockey match during afternoon. Officers v. Sergts. Officers won 7-1.	MM

C.H. Montgomery
Lt. Col.
COMMANDING 17TH (SERVICE) BATN.
THE ROYAL FUSILIERS

www.ingramcontent.com/pod-product-compliance
Lightning Source LLC
Chambersburg PA
CBHW082359170426
43191CB00048B/2117